Declining Labor Force Attachment and Downward Trends in Unemployment and Participation

1 Introduction

The US labor market has witnessed two apparently unrelated secular movements in the last 30 years: a decline in unemployment between the early 1980s and the early 2000s, and a decline in participation since the early 2000s (Figure 1).

Understanding the origins of these secular changes in the labor market is at the center a lively debate among economists and policy makers.[1] An oft-cited explanation is a change in the demographic composition of the population due to the aging of the baby boom generation. Since older workers have lower unemployment and participation rates than younger workers, an older population will have both lower unemployment and participation rates.[2]

In this paper we uncover another, hitherto unnoticed, "composition" effect, which is quantitatively almost as important as demographics in accounting for the long-run behaviors of both unemployment and participation. This effect comes from a change in the characteristics of nonparticipants (individuals outside the labor force): the labor force attachment of nonparticipants declined secularly over the past 35 years, with a particularly strong decline during the second half of the 90s. Using a stock-flow accounting framework, we show that the decline in labor force attachment lowered the unemployment rate by about 0.5 ppt and the participation rate by 1.75 ppt since the late 70s. This is a large effect: in comparison, the widely studied aging of the baby boom lowered unemployment by 0.7 ppt and participation by 1.5 ppt.

A concrete example helps understand how the composition of the nonparticipation pool affects the unemployment rate. Imagine that nonparticipants are of two types. A first type, denoted I for Inactive, has a high utility of non-market activity relative to market work. Typical type I nonparticipants would be retired workers, students, or spouses who take care of their kids. Given their high net utility of non-market activity, type I individuals rarely enter the labor force and when they do, it is often because they were directly offered a (good) job. As a result, when they enter the labor force, they often enter directly through employment. A second group, denoted M for Marginal, has a low utility of non-market activity (relative to market work) and is at the margin of participation. A typical type M individual would be a discouraged worker: someone who used to look for work but recently gave up for lack of opportunities. Because M types are at the margin of participation, small idiosyncratic or

---

[1]See, e.g., Aaronson et al. (2012), Elsby and Shapiro (2012), Moffitt (2012), Sherk (2012), Van Zandweghe (2012), Erceg and Levin (2013), Hotchkiss and Rios-Avila (2013) for recent work on the reasons for the decline in participation. See, e.g., Mortensen and Pissarides (1998), Shimer (1998, 2001), Ball and Moffitt (2002), Hornstein, Krusell, Violante (2007), Pissarides and Vallanti (2007) for recent work on the reasons for long-run movements in unemployment.

[2]The aging of the baby boom generation has been proposed to explain the inverse U-shape movement in unemployment since the early 70s (Perry (1970), Flaim (1979), Gordon (1982), Summers (1986), and Shimer (1998, 2001)).

aggregate shocks can make them switch participation status, i.e., make them switch between nonparticipation and unemployment. As a result, M types move back-and-forth between unemployment and nonparticipation. Because an I type enters the labor force mostly through employment, while an M type enters mostly through unemployment, changes in the composition of the nonparticipation pool affects the unemployment rate. Compared to 30 years ago, the average US nonparticipant is now closer to an I type, i.e., an individual with a high net utility of non-market activity, and this compositional change lowered the unemployment rate.

To capture the degree of labor force attachment of nonparticipants, we use individuals' *desire for work* as an indicator of "proximity" to participation. Nonparticipants are classified as *marginally-attached*, if they desire but are not seeking work, while nonparticipants are considered *inactive* if they neither desire nor are seeking work. Using CPS matched-micro data to construct worker flows between marginal-attachment, inactivity, employment and unemployment, we find that marginally-attached nonparticipants are very likely to enter the labor force in the near future, i.e., are at the margin of participation, while inactive nonparticipants rarely enter the labor force, i.e., are "far" from the participation margin. However, this is not the only difference, and marginally-attached and inactives also display different behaviors when entering the labor force. The marginally-attached enter the labor force mostly through unemployment, while the inactives enter the labor force mainly through employment. Consistent with our illustrative example, this difference in behavior explains why changes in the composition of the nonparticipation pool affects the unemployment rate.

The CPS has been measuring individuals' desire for work consistently since 1976, allowing us to construct a measure of labor force attachment of the nonparticipation pool over 1976-2010. We document a substantial secular decline in the fraction of marginally-attached inside the nonparticipation pool, with a particularly strong decline during the second half of the 90s. Using a stock-flow accounting framework with four labor market states–employment, unemployment, marginally-attachment and inactivity–, we quantify the consequences of this secular trend on the unemployment and participation rates, and we find that lower labor force attachment is the main factor, with demographics, behind the trend in unemployment.

While there has been extensive theoretical work studying how labor demand mechanisms can generate long-run movements in unemployment,[3] the participation decision is a little studied channel.[4] A first implication of our results is that a complete understanding of the trends in unemployment and participation requires a better theoretical understanding of the participation margin and the behavior of individuals at the margin of participation, as recently pursued

---

[3]See Aghion and Howitt 1994, Mortensen and Pissarides 1998, Ball and Moffitt, 2002, Hornstein, Krusell, Violante, 2007, Pissarides and Vallanti, 2007, among others.

[4]A recent exception is Elsby and Shapiro (2012).

by Krusell, Mukoyama, Rogerson and Sahin (2011, 2012).

To help understand the underlying reasons for the downwards trend in labor force attachment and guide the development of possible theories, we provide some additional facts about the decline in the share of marginally-attached.

First, we find that the decline in the share of marginally-attached is not due to a change in the characteristics of nonparticipants, be it demographics (sex, age, education), the structure of the household (e.g., more or fewer kids) or the fraction of nonparticipants in school (if nonparticipants in school were less likely to be at the margin of participation). In other words, the fraction of marginal nonparticipants did not go down, because the number of retired workers, students, or spouses with kids increased. Instead, the fraction of marginal nonparticipants declined for all demographic groups. However, the declines were larger in some groups than in others. The groups most affected by declining attachment are the young, and also, to a lesser extent, women and the less educated. Thus, the decline in labor force attachment appears particularly strong for secondary workers.

Second, we decompose the fraction of marginally-attached, a stock, into its underlying worker flows. We find that the decline in the share of marginal nonparticipants was due to nonparticipants moving away from the labor force. It was not due to marginal nonparticipants moving into the labor force. Going back to our illustrative example, there are now relatively fewer M types in nonparticipation, because some of the M types became I types, not because some of the M types disappeared into the labor force.[5]

A second implication of our results is to contribute to the debate on the measurement of unemployment and on the difficult distinction between the "unemployment" and "nonparticipant" classifications (Clark and Summers 1979, Flinn and Heckman, 1983). While there is no consensus on whether one should include the marginally-attached or not in the definition of unemployment (e.g., Jones and Riddell 1999), we point out a perhaps surprising result: any unemployment measure will be influenced by the presence of marginally-attached, even when the marginally-attached are not counted as unemployed. In some sense, the debate on whether to include or not the marginally-attached in the definition of unemployment is thus irrelevant, because any definition will capture, to some extent, the presence of marginal nonparticipants. Our results point instead towards the need for a close monitoring of the underlying labor market flows in order to assess the state of the labor market.[6]

---

[5]Although helpful for the intuition, this latter statement is a simplification of reality, because the labor market is not static. Instead, flows of workers take place continuously between the different labor market states, so that changes in the share of M types can only be understood by an understanding of the underlying flows. The share of M types declined because of an increase in the propensity of M types to become I and a reduction in the propensity of I types to become M.

[6]This conclusion echoes Juhn, Murphy and Topel (1991, 2002) and Murphy and Topel (1997) who argue that unemployment may not be the best indicator of the state of the labor market, because it excludes persons

By decomposing unemployment into its underlying flows, our paper builds on a large literature, going back at least to Darby, Haltiwanger and Plant (1986), that aims to understand the determinants of unemployment fluctuations by studying the flows of workers in and out of unemployment.[7] However, while the focus of that literature has been exclusively on cyclical frequencies, ours is on secular movements. Moreover, while that literature traditionally takes a two- (Employment and Unemployment) or a three- (Employment, Unemployment and Non-participation) state view of the labor market, we take a four-state view of the labor market, as advocated by Jones and Riddell (1999), that allows us to better capture the time-varying labor force attachment of the nonparticipation pool and quantify the consequences of an, hitherto unnoticed, decline in labor force attachment. While the existence of different degrees of labor force attachment among nonparticipants is well known (Hall 1970, Clark and Summers, 1979), the consequence of a change in labor force attachment on the unemployment rate is, as far as we know, novel. A key lesson of our analysis is that the labor force attachment of nonparticipants can, and did, change over time, with large consequences for aggregate unemployment and participation.[8] Our paper also relates to the heterogeneity hypothesis raised by Darby, Haltiwanger and Plant (1985).[9] The heterogeneity hypothesis posits that changes in the characteristics of the unemployment pool are an important factor behind movements in the unemployment rate. We extend the hypothesis by showing that the characteristics of the nonparticipation pool, in addition to those of the unemployment pool, can also affect the unemployment rate. Finally, and related to the heterogeneity hypothesis, Elsby, Hobijn and Sahin (2013) show that cyclical movements in unemployment can be the result of changes in the number of unemployed at the margin of the labor force. Elsby et al. (2013) focus on the marginal unemployed over the cycle, while we focus on the marginal nonparticipant over the longer-run, but a general conclusion emerges: regardless of the frequency, the behavior of workers at the margin of participation is key to understand changes in the labor market.

Section 2 proposes a measure of the degree of labor force attachment of the nonparticipation pool; Section 3 presents a stock-flow accounting framework to quantify the effect of lower labor force attachment on unemployment and participation; Section 4 discusses the results of the stock-flow decomposition; Section 5 presents additional facts about the downward trend in labor force attachment; Section 6 concludes.

---

who have withdrawn for market driven reasons.

[7] See, among others, Blanchard and Diamond (1989, 1990), Bleakley, Ferris and Fuhrer (1999), Petrongolo and Pissarides (2008), Elsby, Michaels and Solon (2009), Fujita and Ramey (2009), Elsby, Hobijn, and Sahin (2010, 2011, 2013), Hornstein (2012), Shimer (2012).

[8] Although not the focus of this paper, labor market attachment also presents large cyclical fluctuations with the attachment of nonparticipants increasing in recession.

[9] See also Baker (1992), Barnichon and Figura (2013), Elsby et al. (2013).

2 Measuring nonparticipants' attachment to the labor force

Going back at least to Hall (1970), it is well known that there is considerable diversity in the degrees of labor force attachment among nonparticipants: some nonparticipants are "close" to the labor force, i.e., at the margin of participation, while other nonparticipants are "far" from the labor force, i.e., unlikely to enter the labor force in the future.

To capture the degree of labor force attachment of nonparticipants, we use individuals' *desire for work* as an indicator of "proximity" to participation, and in this section, we present a measure of labor force attachment of nonparticipants over 1976-2010. We document a secular decline in labor force attachment over the past 30 years and a particularly strong decline during the second half of the 90s.

2.1 Attachment to the labor force and desire for work

To capture the degree of labor force attachment of nonparticipants, we use "desire for work" as an indicator of "proximity" to participation.

The CPS includes the question "Do you currently want a job now, either full or part-time?" and we use the answer to this question to separate the nonparticipants into two groups; the "Marginally-attached" –individuals who want a job (but are not looking for one)–, denoted M, and the non-marginally attached –individuals who do not want a job (and are not looking for one)–, denoted I, for "Inactive" since these nonparticipants are the furthest away from labor force activity.[10]

To show that "desire for work" conveys information about the likelihood to enter the labor force and future (un)employment status, we use matched-micro data from the CPS over 1994-2010 to construct worker flows and transition rates between marginal-attachment and the labor force, and between inactivity and the labor force.[11]

Figure 2 shows the transition rate from Marginal-attachment to Unemployment (denoted λ^{MU}), the transition rate from Inactivity to Unemployment (denoted λ^{IU}), and, similarly, the transition rates from Marginal-attachment to Employment and from Inactivity to Employment

---

[10] Note that our definition of a marginally-attached is different from that of the BLS, in which a nonparticipant is classified as marginally-attached if he wants to work, is available for work, and has searched for a job in the past year.

[11] See the Appendix for details on the construction of these series, in particular the time-aggregation bias correction. Although the question about "desire for work" was included in the CPS prior to 1994, we can only measure the transition rates in and out of marginal-attachment (or inactivity) after 1994. Since the CPS redesign in 1994, the question "Do you currently want a job now, either full or part-time?" is asked to all rotation groups, allowing us to observe the labor market transitions of the marginally attached, and thus allowing us to measure separate worker flows for marginally-attached and inactives. Before 1994, the question was only asked to the *outgoing* rotation groups and thus does not allow measurement of the underlying flows.

(denoted λ^{ME} and λ^{IE}). Table 1 reports the average values of these transition rates over 1994-2010.

We can see that marginally-attached (M) and inactives (I) display very different transition rates out of nonparticipation. First, a marginally-attached is very likely to enter the labor force in the near future ($\lambda^{MU} + \lambda^{ME} = .62$). In other words, a marginally-attached is at the margin of participation. In contrast, an inactive is unlikely to enter the labor force and is "far" from the participation margin ($\lambda^{IU} + \lambda^{IE} = .05$). Second, while a marginally-attached is much more likely to enter the labor force through unemployment than through employment ($\lambda^{MU} > \lambda^{ME}$), this is exactly the opposite for an inactive. An inactive is much more likely to enter the labor force through employment ($\lambda^{IE} > \lambda^{IU}$). These two differences in behavior between marginal and inactive participants –the fact that $\lambda^{MU} - \lambda^{ME} > 0$ and $\lambda^{IE} - \lambda^{IU} > 0$– will later prove crucial, when we consider the effect of changes in the share of marginally-attached on the unemployment rate.

2.2 A secular decline in attachment to the labor market

We measure the average labor force attachment of the nonparticipation pool with the share of marginally-attached individuals in the nonparticipation pool: the ratio $\frac{M_t}{M_t + I_t}$ with M_t and I_t the respective number of marginally-attached and inactive nonparticipants. Importantly, the phrasing of the CPS question did not change over 1976-2010, allowing us to construct a consistent time-series of the share of marginally-attached individuals in nonparticipation over 1976-2010.[12]

Figure 3 plots the fraction of marginally-attached over 1976-2010 and shows a downward trend in the degree of labor market attachment of the Nonparticipation pool. The trend was especially strong in the second half of the 90s.

Since marginally-attached and inactives display very different transition rates into employment and unemployment, a change in the composition of the nonparticipation pool could affect the transition rates out of nonparticipation and thus generate movements in the unemployment and participation rates. In the next section, we quantify the consequences of lower labor force attachment on the unemployment and participation rates.

---

[12]While the "desire for work" question is asked to all rotation groups after 1994, it is only asked to the outgoing rotation groups before 1994, i.e., 1/4 of the sample. We verified that this difference did not affect our measurement, by calculating the fraction of marginally-attached using only the outgoing rotation groups over the whole sample 1976-2010, and compared it with our main measure. Although this alternative measure is more noisy, the two series behave remarkably similarly after 1994.

3 An accounting framework to quantify the effect of lower labor force attachment on unemployment and participation

In this section, we present an accounting framework to quantify the effect of the decline in the share of marginally-attached on the unemployment and participation rates. Because changes in the demographics structure of the population are known to have large effects on the behavior of the unemployment and participation rates, we develop an accounting framework that controls for changes in demographics.

3.1 Lower labor force attachment and transition rates out of Nonparticipation

Because marginally-attached and inactives have different propensities to join employment and unemployment, changes in the fraction of marginally-attached will affect the average transition rates out of Nonparticipation (denoted N).

Specifically, the transition rate from Nonparticipation to Unemployment (denoted λ^{NU}) and the transition rate from Nonparticipation to Employment (denoted λ^{NE}) are weighted averages of the two group specific transition rates and satisfy

$$\begin{cases} \lambda_t^{NU} = \left(\frac{M}{N}\right)_t \lambda_t^{MU} + \left(1 - \left(\frac{M}{N}\right)_t\right) \lambda_t^{IU} \\ \lambda_t^{NE} = \left(\frac{M}{N}\right)_t \lambda_t^{ME} + \left(1 - \left(\frac{M}{N}\right)_t\right) \lambda_t^{IE} \end{cases} . \tag{1}$$

In order to quantify the effect of the decline in the share of marginally-attached on the unemployment and participation rates, we thus need to relate changes in the transition rates out of Nonparticipation to movements in the unemployment and participation rates. To do so, we now present a stock-flow model of the labor market.

3.2 The basic stock-flow model of the labor market

The unemployment and participation rates are stocks determined by underlying labor market flows, describing how workers transit between different labor market states. With the labor market described by three labor market states –Employment (E), Unemployment (U) and Nonparticipation (N)–,[13] the numbers of unemployed, employed and nonparticipants satisfy

---

[13] Non-employed individuals are defined as unemployed when they are actively searching for a job, while non-employed individuals are considered nonparticipants when they are not actively searching for a job.

the system of differential equations

$$
\begin{pmatrix} \dot{E} \\ U \\ N \end{pmatrix}_t = \begin{pmatrix} 1 - \lambda^{EU} - \lambda^{EN} & \lambda^{UE} & \lambda^{NE} \\ \lambda^{EU} & 1 - \lambda^{UE} - \lambda^{UN} & \lambda^{NU} \\ \lambda^{EN} & \lambda^{UN} & 1 - \lambda^{NU} - \lambda^{NE} \end{pmatrix}_t \begin{pmatrix} E \\ U \\ N \end{pmatrix}_t \quad (2)
$$

where λ_t^{AB} denotes the hazard rate of transiting from state $A \in \{E, U, N\}$ to state $B \in \{E, U, N\}$.

Figure 4 plots the behavior of the six aggregate transition rates over 1976-2010.[14] It reveals a striking, and as far as we know previously unnoticed, downward trend in the rate at which nonparticipants individuals enter unemployment (λ^{NU}).[15] Between the two business cycle peaks of 1979 and 2006, λ^{NU} declined by 30 percent. Interestingly, this decline is consistent with the downward trend in labor force attachment documented in the previous section: since marginally-attached are much more likely to join unemployment than inactives, a decline in the share of marginally-attached will generate a decline in λ^{NU}.

3.3 An accounting framework with demographic changes

Changes in the demographics structure of the population are known to have large effects on the behavior of the unemployment and participation rates. We now present an accounting framework that controls for demographics and allows us to quantify the contribution of the different transition rates to movements in unemployment and participation.

We divide the population into K demographic (age and sex) groups. In each group, workers can be in one of three labor market states: employment (E), unemployment (U) and nonparticipation (N). We refer to a demographic group i with a subscript i. For instance, U_{it}, E_{it}, and N_{it} denote the number of unemployed, employed and nonparticipants, respectively, in group i at instant t, and similarly for the transition rates. The behavior of U_{it}, E_{it}, and N_{it} is described by the same system (2), only indexed by i.

Our accounting framework is based on a steady-state assumption, as in Shimer (2012). At a quarterly frequency, the unemployment rate $u_{it} = \frac{U_{it}}{LF_{it}}$ with $LF_{it} = E_{it} + U_{it}$ is very well

---

[14] See the Appendix for details on the construction of these series, in particular the correction for the 1994 CPS redesign and the time-aggregation bias correction.

[15] Two other flows display remarkable trends. First, the job separation rate (Employment-Unemployment transition rate) experienced a secular decline over the last thirty years, as previously discussed in e.g., Davis (2008). Second, the Employment-Nonparticipation transition rate displayed a secular decline up until the early 1990s, a trend that Abraham and Shimer (2001) attributed to the rise in women's labor force attachment until the early 90s.

approximated by its steady-state value u_{it}^{ss} so that we can use the accounting identity[16]

$$u_{it} \simeq u_{it}^{ss} \equiv \frac{s_{it}}{s_{it} + f_{it}} \tag{3}$$

where s_{it} and f_{it} are

$$\begin{cases} f_{it} = \lambda_{it}^{UE} + \lambda_{it}^{UN} \frac{\lambda_{it}^{NE}}{\lambda_{it}^{NE} + \lambda_{it}^{NU}} \\ s_{it} = \lambda_{it}^{EU} + \lambda_{it}^{EN} \frac{\lambda_{it}^{NU}}{\lambda_{it}^{NE} + \lambda_{it}^{NU}} \end{cases} . \tag{4}$$

Similarly, the steady-state of system (2) provides an accounting identity for the labor force participation rate of each demographic group. The labor force participation rate is $l_{it} = \frac{LF_{it}}{Pop_{it}}$ with Pop_{it} the number of individuals of type i in the working-age population. A little bit of algebra gives

$$\begin{aligned} l_{it} &\equiv \frac{U_{it} + E_{it}}{Pop_{it}} \\ &\simeq l_{it}^{ss} = \frac{s_{it} + f_{it}}{s_{it} + f_{it} + \frac{\lambda_{it}^{EU} \lambda_{it}^{UN} + \lambda_{it}^{UE} \lambda_{it}^{EN} + \lambda_{it}^{UN} \lambda_{it}^{EN}}{\lambda_{it}^{NE} + \lambda_{it}^{NU}}} . \end{aligned} \tag{5}$$

Denoting $\omega_{it} = \frac{LF_{it}}{LF_t}$ the share of group $i \in \{1, .., K\}$ in the labor force and $\Omega_{it} = \frac{Pop_{it}}{Pop_t}$ the population share of group i, we can combine the accounting identities for the unemployment rate (3) and labor force participation rate (5) of each demographic group and aggregate across groups using:[17]

$$\begin{cases} u_t = \sum_{i=1}^{K} \omega_{it} u_{it} = \sum_{i=1}^{K} \Omega_{it} \frac{l_{it}}{l_t} u_{it} \\ l_t = \sum_{i=1}^{K} \Omega_{it} l_{it} \end{cases} \tag{6}$$

The two identities (6) are functions of the six hazard rates of each demographic group (the λ_{it}^{AB}s, $A, B \in \{E, U, N\}$, $i \in \{1, .., K\}$) and functions of the population shares (Ω_{it}, $i \in \{1, .., K\}$) of each group.

By taking a Taylor expansion of the identities (6) around the mean of the hazard rates of each demographic group i ($\lambda_{it}^{AB} \simeq \lambda_i^{AB} \equiv E\lambda_{it}^{AB}$) and around the mean of the population share ($\Omega_{it} \simeq \Omega_i \equiv E\Omega_{it}$) of each group, we can decompose the aggregate unemployment rate u_t and labor force participation rate l_t into the contribution of changes in demographics and

---

[16]In the U.S., the magnitudes of the hazard rates are such that the half-life of a deviation of unemployment from its steady state value is about one month (Shimer, 2012).

[17]Note that $\omega_{it} = \frac{l_{it}}{l_t} \Omega_{it}$, so that ω_{it} is also a function of the underlying worker flows.

the contributions of movements in each transition rate:[18]

$$\begin{cases} du_t = du_t^{\Omega} + du_t^{UE} + du_t^{UN} + du_t^{EU} + du_t^{EN} + du_t^{NU} + du_t^{NE} + \varepsilon_t^u \\ dl_t = dl_t^{\Omega} + dl_t^{UE} + dl_t^{UN} + dl_t^{EU} + dl_t^{EN} + dl_t^{NU} + dl_t^{NE} + \varepsilon_t^l \end{cases} \tag{7}$$

with $du_t^{\Omega} = \sum_{i=1}^{K} \beta_i^{\Omega} (\Omega_{it} - \Omega_i)$ capturing the contribution of demographics

and $du_t^{AB} = \sum_{i=1}^{K} \beta_i^{AB} (\lambda_{it}^{AB} - \lambda_i^{AB})$, $A, B \in \{E, U, N\}$, β_i^{AB} the coefficients of the Taylor expansion, capturing the contribution of λ^{AB}, the transition rate from A to B to the unemployment rate (holding the demographic structure of the population constant). ε_t^u is the Taylor approximation error. Similar notations apply to the decomposition of the labor force participation rate.

3.4 Quantifying the effect of lower labor force attachment on unemployment and participation

We can now quantify the effect of changes in the share of marginally-attached on the unemployment and participation rates.

From the accounting decomposition (7), the effect of the transitions out of nonparticipation on the unemployment rate is given by:[19]

$$\begin{aligned} du_t^{NU} + du_t^{NE} &= \sum_{i=1}^{K} \beta_i^{NU} (\lambda_{it}^{NU} - \lambda_i^{NU}) + \sum_{i=1}^{K} \beta_i^{NE} (\lambda_{it}^{NE} - \lambda_i^{NE}) \\ &= \sum_{i=1}^{K} \beta_i^{NU} \left((\lambda_{it}^{NU} - \lambda_i^{NU}) - \frac{\lambda_i^{NU}}{\lambda_i^{NE}} (\lambda_{it}^{NE} - \lambda_i^{NE}) \right) \end{aligned} \tag{8}$$

where we used the fact that $\beta_i^{NE} = -\beta_i^{NU} \frac{\lambda_i^{NU}}{\lambda_i^{NE}}$.[20] With $\beta_i^{NU} > 0$ and $\beta_i^{NE} < 0$, an increase in the transition rate from Nonparticipation to Unemployment raises the unemployment rate

---

[18] By taking a Taylor expansion around the mean, instead of around an HP-filter trend or around last period's value as in Elsby et al. (2009) or Fujita and Ramey (2009), our decomposition has the advantage of covering all frequencies and hence allows us to analyze low-frequency movements. While our notation may suggest a first-order expansion, this is only done for clarity of exposition. To guarantee that the approximation remains good however, we take a second-order approximation, which performs extremely well, as we show in the Appendix. The coefficients of the Taylor expansion are available upon request. The cross-order terms were split equally between any two components.

[19] Again, the decomposition is presented as a first-order Taylor expansion for ease of exposition, but the quantitative results are based on the 2nd-order Taylor expansion.

[20] This comes out of the Taylor expansion with $\beta^{NU} = \frac{\lambda^{NE}(\lambda^{EN}\lambda^{UE} + \lambda^{UN}(\lambda^{EN} + \lambda^{EU}))}{(\lambda^{EU}\lambda^{IE} + \lambda^{EN}\lambda^{NU} + \lambda^{EU}\lambda^{NU} + \lambda^{NE}\lambda^{UE} + \lambda^{NE}\lambda^{UN} + \lambda^{IU}\lambda^{UE})^2}$
(omitting the i subscript).

$(\beta_i^{NU} > 0)$, whereas an increase in the transition rate from Nonparticipation to Employment lowers the unemployment rate $(\beta_i^{NE} < 0)$.

Differencing (1) for each demographic group and combining with (8), we obtain the effect of a change in the fraction of marginally-attached on the aggregate unemployment rate, denoted $du_t^{M/N}$:

$$du_t^{M/N} = \sum_{i=1}^{N} \beta_i^{NU} \left[\left(\lambda_i^{MU} - \lambda_i^{IU} \right) - \frac{\lambda_i^{NU}}{\lambda_i^{NE}} \left(\lambda_i^{ME} - \lambda_i^{IE} \right) \right] d \left(\frac{M}{N} \right)_{it} \qquad (9)$$

with $\left(\frac{M}{N} \right)_{it}$ the fraction of marginally-attached nonparticipants in demographic group i at time t.

From (9), we can see that the effect of a decline in labor force attachment on the aggregate unemployment rate is a priori ambiguous. On the one hand, as captured by the first term on the right-hand side of (9), a decline in $\frac{M}{N}$ lowers the average NU transition rate since marginally-attached are more likely to join unemployment than inactives $(\lambda_i^{MU} - \lambda_i^{IU} > 0)$, and this lowers the unemployment rate. On the other hand, as captured by the second term on the right-hand side of (9), a decline in $\frac{M}{N}$ lowers the average N-E transition rate, since marginally-attached are also more likely to join employment $(\lambda_i^{ME} - \lambda_i^{IE} > 0)$, and this increases the unemployment rate.

To quantify the effect of lower labor force attachment on the participation rate, we proceed in the exact same fashion and calculate $dl_t^{M/N}$, the effect of changes in the fraction of marginally-attached on the labor force participation rate from a relation similar to (9). Contrary to the unemployment rate, a decline in the fraction of marginally attached has a clear effect on the labor force participation rate. Since a lower fraction of marginally attached lowers all transition rates out of Nonparticipation, a lower fraction of marginally attached implies a lower labor force participation rate.

4 Decomposition results

We now present the results of the stock-flow decompositions of the unemployment and participation rates. We find that the decline in the labor force attachment of nonparticipants generated substantial downward trends in unemployment and participation. In fact, lower labor force attachment is the main factor, with demographics, behind the trend in unemployment.

4.1 Decomposition of the unemployment rate

Figure 5 plots the contribution of changes in demographics and labor market flows (transitions out of Nonparticipation, Employment and Unemployment) to the aggregate unemployment rate. In the middle-upper panel, along with the contribution of the flows out of Nonparticipation, Figure 5 plots $du_t^{M/N}$, the contribution of changes in the fraction of marginally-attached to the unemployment rate.[21]

The decline in the fraction of marginally-attached, $du_t^{M/N}$ (middle-upper panel, dashed line), *lowered* the aggregate unemployment rate and accounts for most of the downward trend in unemployment due to the flows out of Nonparticipation (middle-upper panel, solid line). The contribution of $du_t^{M/N}$ is substantial and on a par with demographics. Comparing the business cycle peaks of 1979 and 2006, the decline in labor force attachment lowered the unemployment rate by about 0.5 ppt over the last 30 years. In comparison, demographics and the aging of the population, an oft-cited reason for the trend in unemployment, lowered unemployment by about 0.7 percentage point. Other transition rates only played a marginal role. Despite the abundant literature that emphasized the decline in the job separation rate and turn-over rate (e.g., Davis, 2008, Fujita, 2012), after adjusting for demographics, transitions out of Employment (including the contributions of both the EN and EU transition rates) only lowered unemployment by about 0.15 percentage point between 1979 and 2006. Transitions out of unemployment lowered unemployment by about 0.2 percentage point.

To help understand why a lower share of marginally-attached unambiguously implies a lower unemployment rate, we can go back to (9). In practice, the two hazard rates out of nonparticipation, λ_i^{NU} and λ_i^{NE}, are of similar magnitudes and $\frac{\lambda_i^{NU}}{\lambda_i^{NE}} \simeq 1$ (see Figure 4 for the aggregate case). As a result, the sign of the effect of a change in $\frac{M}{N}$ on the unemployment rate is given by (rearranging (9) a little and omitting the demographic subscript for clarity)

$$\underbrace{\left(\lambda^{MU} - \lambda^{ME}\right)}_{>0} + \underbrace{\left(\lambda^{IE} - \lambda^{IU}\right)}_{>0} > 0$$

which is unambiguously positive for two reasons: (i) a marginally-attached enters the labor force mainly through unemployment ($\lambda^{MU} - \lambda^{ME} > 0$), and (ii) an inactive enters the labor force mostly through employment ($\lambda^{IE} - \lambda^{IU} > 0$).

---

[21] The contribution of the flows out of Nonparticipation is the contribution of NU and NE flows given by (8), and it *includes* the contribution $du_t^{M/N}$.

4.2 Decomposition of the labor force participation rate

Figure 6 plots the contribution of demographics and labor market flows (transitions out of Nonparticipation, Employment and Unemployment) to the aggregate participation rate. In the middle-upper panel, along with the contribution of the flows out of Nonparticipation, Figure 5 plots $dl_t^{M/N}$, the contribution of changes in the fraction of marginally-attached to the participation rate.

The decline in the fraction of marginally-attached lowered the labor force participation rate by $1\frac{3}{4}$ ppt since the late 70s. Again, this is a large effect. Over the same time period, demographics and the aging of the population lowered participation by $1\frac{1}{2}$ ppt.[22]

Interestingly, this result implies that part of the explanation for the currently low level of participation should be traced back to the mid-90s, when labor market attachment started its abrupt decline, and not necessarily to the early 2000s (the focus of recent work, e.g., Moffitt, 2012), which marks the beginning of the secular decline in participation (Figure 1).

The decline in labor force attachment did not translate immediately into lower labor force participation, because it was offset by upward pressures on the participation rate in the late second half of the 90s coming from increases in the job finding rates out of unemployment (UE, Figure 4 upper-panel and Figure 6 lower panel) and out of nonparticipation (NE, Figure 4 lower panel and Figure 6, upper-middle panel).[23] Thus, even though labor market attachment started its declined long before the early 2000s, that secular decline appears to have been masked (from the perspective of the labor force participation rate) by the strong labor demand of the late 90s.

5 A change in the characteristics of nonparticipants ?

We showed that the decline in the share of marginally-attached nonparticipants had a major impact on the unemployment and participation rates. In this section, we investigate whether the decline was due to a change in the observable characteristics of nonparticipants. Using CPS micro data to control for worker characteristics, we find that changes in the characteristics of nonparticipants cannot explain the lower share of marginally attached nonparticipants. The

---

[22] Another noteworthy trend is the contribution of transitions out employment (Figure 6, lower middle panel). While that trend was initially driven by women's decreasing rate of labor force exit from employment, λ^{EN}, (Abraham and Shimer, 2001), since the early 2000s, that trend is driven by old workers' decreasing rate of labor force exit from employment (λ^{EN}), as old workers postpone retirement (the hazard rates by demographic groups are available upon request). The higher labor force attachment of older workers almost completely cancels out the effect of population aging on the participation rate.

[23] Employed workers are much less likely to leave the labor force than unemployed workers. As a result, by raising the number of employed workers relative to the number of unemployed workers, an increase in the UE rate increases the labor force participation rate.

decline in labor force attachment was broad based across worker groups, but particularly strong for the young, and to a lesser extent, women and the less-educated.

5.1 Specification

To explore whether changes in the composition of the Nonparticipation pool can account for the decline in the fraction of marginally-attached, we estimate a linear probability model of nonparticipants' propensity to want a job. Specifically, the probability of a nonparticipant of type i to want a job (i.e., be M) at time t is given by

$$P(M|N)_{it} = \beta_t X_{it} + \varepsilon_{it} \tag{10}$$

with X_{it} a vector of characteristics for type i at time t, and where the coefficients β_t are allowed to change from year to year.[24]

We can then isolate the contribution of composition to the change in the share of marginally-attached between 1994 and 2010 from

$$\left(\frac{M}{N}\right)_{10} - \left(\frac{M}{N}\right)_{94} = \underbrace{\beta_{94}\left(\bar{X}_{10} - \bar{X}_{94}\right)}_{\text{Composition effect}} + \bar{X}_{10}\left(\beta_{10} - \beta_{94}\right)$$

with $\bar{X}_t$ the average worker characteristics in year t, $\bar{X}_t = \sum_i \varpi_{it} X_{it}$ with ϖ_{it} the share of nonparticipant of type i at time t.

Using CPS micro data over 1994-2010, we control for the following characteristics (i) age group –we classify workers into 8 groups spanning 16-85–, (ii) sex, (iii) education level –less than high school, high school or some college, college or more–, (iv) school status –in school or not–, and (v) position in household –head, spouse, child, other–.

The number of nonparticipants going to school has increased continuously over the past 15 years (Figure 7). If individuals going to school are less likely to want a job, the increase in school attendance could explain the decline in labor force attachment. We thus include school status in the regression to test for this possibility. We also included position in household to test whether a change in the composition of households may be behind the decline in labor force attachment.

5.2 Coefficient estimates

Figure 8 presents our coefficient estimates. For ease of comparison, the coefficients are expressed in units of probability to want a job. Not surprisingly, individuals with the highest

---

[24] We use data at a yearly frequency, estimating β_t from cross-sectional variation during the year t.

expected lifetime return from work are the most likely to want to work: young, highly educated, men are the most likely to want to work. In line with our earlier intuition, being in school substantially lowers the desire for work.

5.3   Composition effect

Table 2 shows that changes in demographics, in the fraction of nonparticipants in school or in the structure of the household cannot explain the decline in labor force attachment.

In fact, changes in observable characteristics alone would have led to a small increase in the fraction of marginally attached. While the population is now older, which might lead one to expect a positive contribution from composition, changes in the age composition of nonparticipants actually acted to increase the share of the marginally attached. This somewhat counterintuitive result is explained by the secular increase in the labor force participation of 55+ workers, which led the share of 55+ workers in Nonparticipation to decrease. Since older workers are less attached to the labor force, this compositional change increased the average labor force attachment of Nonparticipation.[25]

5.4   Changes in coefficients

The decline in the share of marginally-attached thus appears to capture a decline in individuals' attachment to the labor force. To highlight the categories most affected by the change in labor force attachment, Figure 9 plots the relative changes in the estimated coefficients, the vector β_t, between 2010 and 1994. We can see that the decline in labor force attachment was widespread across groups. However, the declines were larger in some groups than in other. The groups most affected by declining attachment are the young, and also, to a lesser extent, women and the less educated. Thus, the decline in labor force attachment appears particularly strong for secondary workers.

Figure 10 shows the same result from a slightly different angle: it plots the fraction of marginally-attached among nonparticipants for four demographic subgroups: Prime-age male 25-55, Prime-age female 25-55, Younger than 25 and Over 55. The secular decline in labor force attachment is strongest for young workers, and to a lesser extent prime-age women. Moreover, for young workers, the secular decline appears to go back to the early 80s, pointing to an even older phenomenon.

---

[25] While the increase in the fraction of nonparticipants in school time did decrease labor force attachment, the effect is quantitatively too small to matter. Changes in the household structure were too small to have an effect.

6 A stock-flow decomposition of $\frac{M}{N}$

The fraction of marginally-attached is a stock, and, as such, its movements are difficult to interpret, because changes in a stock are the results of simultaneous, and possibly offsetting, movements in the underlying flows (what Elsby et al., 2013 refer to as a stock-flow fallacy).

To address this possible issue, we use a four state stock-flow model of the labor market to decompose the fraction of marginally-attached nonparticipants, a stock, into its underlying flows. We show that the decline in the fraction of marginally-attached in the second half of the 90s was due to nonparticipants moving *away from the labor force*. It was not due to marginal nonparticipants moving into the labor force.[26]

To do so, we generalize our stock-flow model of the labor market to four states: employment, unemployment, marginal-attachment and inactivity, and the number of employed E_t, unemployed U_t, marginally-attached M_t and inactives I_t satisfy the system

$$\begin{pmatrix} \overset{\bullet}{E} \\ U \\ M \\ I \end{pmatrix}_t = L_t \begin{pmatrix} E \\ U \\ M \\ I \end{pmatrix}_t \tag{11}$$

with

$$L_t = \begin{pmatrix} 1 - \lambda^{EU} - \lambda^{EM} - \lambda^{EI} & \lambda^{UE} & \lambda^{ME} & \lambda^{IE} \\ \lambda^{EU} & 1 - \lambda^{UE} - \lambda^{UM} - \lambda^{UI} & \lambda^{MU} & \lambda^{IU} \\ \lambda^{EM} & \lambda^{UM} & 1 - \lambda^{MU} - \lambda^{ME} - \lambda^{MI} & \lambda^{IM} \\ \lambda^{EI} & \lambda^{UI} & \lambda^{MI} & 1 - \lambda^{IU} - \lambda^{IE} - \lambda^{IM} \end{pmatrix}_t$$

and λ^{AB} the hazard rate of transiting between states A and B. As detailed in the Appendix, using the steady-state of this system, we can obtain an accounting identity for any stock variable, and in this case, express the fraction of marginally-attached $\frac{M}{N}$ as a function of the 12 hazard rates. Taking a Taylor expansion around the mean of the hazard rates, we get a decomposition of $\frac{M}{N}$ movements with

$$d\left(\frac{M}{N}\right)_t \simeq \sum_{A \neq B} \gamma^{AB} d\lambda_t^{AB} \tag{12}$$

with $A, B \in \{E, U, M, I\}$ and $\{\gamma^{AB}\}$ the coefficients of the Taylor expansion.[27]

---

[26] Or to other more mechanical effects. For instance, a decline in the ratio of unemployed to employed could mechanically lower $\frac{M}{N}$, if unemployed workers are more likely to become marginally-attached than employed workers.

[27] While (12) is presented for the aggregate hazard rates for clarity of exposition, the relation holds for each

While decomposition (12) can appear cumbersome, our results are surprisingly simple, and we find that two hazard rates account for most of the behavior of $\frac{M}{N}$ since the mid-90s: λ^{IM} and λ^{MI}.

Using (12), we can assess the separate contributions of each hazard rate by noting as in Fujita and Ramey (2009) that $Var\,(y+z) = Cov(y,y+z) + Cov(z,y+z)$ with $y,z \in \mathbb{R}$ so that, for example, $\frac{Cov(\gamma^{MI}d\lambda_t^{MI}, d(\frac{M}{N})_t)}{Var(d(\frac{M}{N})_t)}$ measures the fraction of the variance of $\frac{M}{N}$ due to changes in the MI transition rate.

The variance decomposition exercise shows that λ^{IM} and λ^{MI} account for, respectively, 50% and 25% of the variance of $\frac{M}{N}$ (Table 3).[28] Figure 11 plots M/N over 1994-2010 along with the movements in M/N generated solely by movements in λ^{MI} and λ^{IM}. We can see that these two hazard rates account for most of the downward trend in $\frac{M_t}{I_t}$ since 1994.

In words, the decline in the fraction of marginally attached was caused by a reduction in the propensity of inactives to become marginally attached (λ^{IM} declined, Figure 12) and an increase in the propensity of marginally attached to become inactive (λ^{MI} increased, Figure 12). We conclude that the decline in the share of marginal nonparticipants was due to nonparticipants moving further away from the labor force. It was not due to nonparticipants moving into the labor force and into employment.

Since the decline in labor force attachment was strongest for the young, Table 3 shows the results of the same stock-flow decomposition applied only to the less than 25 and comes to the same conclusion. Transitions between marginal-attachment and inactivity account for 77 % of the variance of $\frac{M}{N}$, and as shown in Figure 13, movements in λ^{MI} and λ^{IM} (shown in Figure 14) account for virtually all of the downward trend in labor force attachment. Again, the decline in the share of marginal young nonparticipants was due to young nonparticipants moving further away from the labor force.

7 Conclusion and discussion

This paper uncovers a new factor behind the trends in unemployment and participation over the past 30 years. The share of nonparticipants at the margin of participation declined secularly over the past 35 years, with a particularly strong decline in the second-half of the 90s.

Using CPS matched-micro data and a stock-flow accounting framework, we quantify the effect of that decline on aggregate labor market variables and find that the unemployment rate was lowered by about 0.5 ppt and the participation rate by about 1.75 ppt. This is a large

---

demographic group.

[28] While the variance decomposition reported in Table 3 is for unfiltered data, the variance decomposition is similar at low and cyclical frequencies.

effect. In comparison, the widely studied aging of the baby boom lowered unemployment by 0.7 ppt and participation by 1.5 ppt.

The effect of changes in labor force attachment on unemployment comes from the fact that marginal nonparticipants behave very differently from other nonparticipants when entering the labor force: marginal nonparticipants enter mostly through unemployment, while other nonparticipants enter mostly through employment. We conclude that a complete understanding of the trends in unemployment and participation requires a better understanding of the participation margin, as recently pursued in Krusell et al. (2011, 2012).

Understanding the reasons for the decline in labor force attachment is an important task for future research. We show that the downward trend in the share of marginally-attached was broad-based across demographic groups, but particularly strong for the young and, although to a lesser extent, secondary workers in general. Moreover, the decline in the share of marginal nonparticipants was due to nonparticipants moving away from the labor force. We hypothesize that two forces could have led to a decline in labor force attachment: (i) an inward shift of the labor supply curve concentrated among the young, and/or (ii) a reduction in labor demand concentrated among the young.

An inward labor supply shift could have been caused by a reduction in the added-worker effect driven by the strong wage growth in the second half of the 90s.[29] Secondary workers would have become less interested in working, because the primary worker (the main income earner) saw his real wage increase significantly after the mid-90s. Supporting this hypothesis, Figure 15 plots the real median family income over 1976-2010 along with the fraction of marginally attached (on a negative scale) and shows a striking correlation, suggesting a possible role for the added-worker effect.[30] Alternatively, an inward labor supply shift could have been caused by a higher emphasis on education, perhaps in part in response to a rising high school and college wage premium, which has increased the incentives to be in school rather than in the labor force (see, e.g., Aaronson, Park, and Sullivan 2006). This incentive would have been particularly strong for young and very young nonparticipants (between 16 and 19), in line with our evidence that the decline in labor force attachment was strongest for teens. Finally, an inward labor demand shift could have been caused by increased trade competition (as recently argued by Autor, Dorn and Hanson, 2013) or increased competition from immigrants, which was shown to have strongly affected the young (Smith, 2012).[31] Exploring these hypotheses is

---

[29] The added-worker effect (Lundberg, 1985, Juhn and Potter, 2007) refers to the mechanism through which the secondary worker(s) in a household can be more or less likely to want to work (or more generally participate in the labor market) depending on the labor market status and income of the household's primary worker.

[30] Data on family income are taken from CPS Annual Social and Economic Supplement microdata. Data are inflated to 2011 dollars using the CPI-U-RS. Using instead real earnings per hour from the CPS Merged Outgoing Rotation Group gives a similar result.

[31] Particularly interesting is Autor et al. (2013) conclusion that the effect of trade competition does not show

an important goal for future research.

---

up as much as a rise in the unemployment rate as it does in a decline in labor-force participation, consistent with a decline in labor force attachment.

20

References

[1] Aaronson, Daniel, Kyung-Hong Park, and Daniel Sullivan. 2006. The decline in teen labor force participation. Economic Perspectives 2-18, 2006.

[2] Aaronson, Daniel, Jonathan Davis, and Luojia Hu. 2012. "Explaining the Decline in the U.S. Labor Force Participation Rate." FRB Chicago, Chicago Fed Letter 296 (March).

[3] Autor, D., D. Dorn, and G. Hanson. "Trade, Technology and the Labor Market," NBER WorkingPaper, 2013.

[4] Abraham, K. and R. Shimer. "Changes in Unemployment Duration and Labor-Force Attachment." in The Roaring Nineties, Russell Sage Foundation, 2002.

[5] Barnichon, R. and A. Figura. "Labor Market Heterogeneities, and the Aggregate Matching Function," mimeo, 2013.

[6] Ball, L. and R. Moffit,. "Productivity growth and the Phillips curve," in The Roaring Nineties, Russell Sage Foundation, 2002.

[7] Blanchard O. and P. Diamond. "The Beveridge Curve," *Brookings Paper on Economic Activity*, 1:1-60, 1989.

[8] Blanchard O. and P. Diamond. "The Cyclical Behavior of the Gross Flows of U.S. Workers," *Brookings Papers on Economic Activity*, vol. 21(2), 85-156, 1990.

[9] Bleakley H., A. Ferris, and J. Fuhrer "New Data on Worker Flows during Business Cycles," *New England Economic Review*, July-August, 1999.

[10] Clark, K. and L. Summers. "Labor Market Dynamics and Unemployment: A Reconsideration." Brookings Papers on Economic Activity, (1): 13-60 1979.

[11] Darby, M. J. Haltiwanger and M. Plant. "The Ins and Outs of Unemployment: The Ins Win," NBER Working Paper, 1986.

[12] Davis, S. "The Decline of Job Loss and Why It Matters," *American Economic Review Papers and Proceedings*, 2008.

[13] Elsby, M., B. Hobijn and A. Sahin. "The Labor Market in the Great Recession," *Brookings Papers on Economic Activity*, 1-48, 2010.

[14] Elsby, M. B. Hobijn and A. Sahin. "Unemployment Dynamics in the OECD," Working Paper, 2011.

[15] Elsby, M. B. Hobijn and A. Sahin. "On the Importance of the Participation Margin for Labor Market Fluctuations," Working Paper, 2013.

[16] Elsby, M. R. Michaels and G. Solon. "The Ins and Outs of Cyclical Unemployment," *American Economic Journal: Macroeconomics,* 2009.

[17] Elsby, M. and M. Shapiro. "Why Does Trend Growth Affect Equilibrium Employment? A New Explanation of an Old Puzzle," *American Economic Review,* June 2012.

[18] Erceg, C. and A. Levin. "Labor Force Participation and Monetary Policy in the Wake of the Great Recession," Working Paper 2013.

[19] Flaim, P. "The Effect of Demographic Changes on the Nation's Unemployment Rate," *Monthly Labor Review,* 3-10, 1979.

[20] Flinn, C. and J. Heckman. "Are Unemployment and Out of the Labor Force Behaviorally Distinct Labor Force States?," *Journal of Labor Economics,* vol. 1(1), pages 28-42, 1983.

[21] Fujita, S. "Declining Labor Turnover and Turbulence," Working Paper 11-44, 2012.

[22] Fujita, S. and G. Ramey. "The Cyclicality of Separation and Job Finding Rates," *International Economic Review,* 2009.

[23] Gordon, R. Inflation, flexible exchange rates, and the natural rate of unemployment. In Workers, Jobs and Inflation, Brookings Institute, 89-152, 1982.

[24] Hall, R. "Why is the unemployment rate so high at full employment" *Brookings Papers onEconomic Activity,* 33:369-402, 1970.

[25] Hornstein, A. "Accounting for Unemployment: The Long and Short of It," Working Paper, 2012.

[26] Hornstein, A., P. Krusell and G. Violante "Technology-Policy Interaction in Frictional Labour-Markets," *Review of Economic Studies,* 74(4), 1089-1124, 2007.

[27] Hotchkiss, J., Pitts, M., Rios-Avila, F. 2012. "A Closer Look at Non-Participants during and after the Great Recession." Federal Reserve Bank of Atlanta Working Paper No.2012-10.

[28] Jones, S. and C. Riddell. "The Measurement of Unemployment: An Empirical Approach," *Econometrica,* 67, pp 142-167, 1999.

[29] Juhn, C., K. Murphy and R. Topel. "Why has the Natural Rate Increased over Time," *Brookings Papers on Economic Activity,* (2) pp75-142, 1991.

[30] Juhn, C., K. Murphy, R. Topel. "Current Unemployment, Historically Contemplated." *Brookings Papers on Economic Activity*, 79-116, 2002.

[31] Juhn, C. and S. Potter "Is There Still an Added-Worker Effect?," NBER Working aper, 2007.

[32] Krusell, P., T. Mukoyama, R. Rogerson, A.Sahin, "A Three State Model of Worker Flows in General Equilibrium," *Journal of Economic Theory* 146, 1107-1133, 2011.

[33] Krusell, P., T. Mukoyama, R. Rogerson, A.Sahin, "Gross Worker Flows over the Business Cycle," Working Paper, 2012.

[34] Lundberg, S. "The Added Worker Effect", *Journal of Labor Economics*, 3(1), 11–37, 1985.

[35] Mortensen, D and C. Pissarides. "Technological Progress, Job Creation, and Job Destruction", *Review of Economic Dynamics*, 1 (4), 733–753, 1998.

[36] Perry, G. "Changing Labor Markets and Inflation," *Brookings Papers on Economic Activity*, 411-441, 1970.

[37] Pissarides, C. and G. Vallanti. "The Impact of TFP Growth on Steady-State Unemployment." *International Economic Review* 48 607-640, 2007.

[38] Petrongolo, B. and C. Pissarides. "Looking into the black box: A survey of the matching function," *Journal of Economic Literature*, 39: 390-431, 2001.

[39] Petrongolo, B., and C. Pissarides. "The Ins and Outs of European Unemployment." *American Economic Review*, 98(2): 256–62, 2008.

[40] Poterba, J. and L. Summers "Reporting Errors and Labor Market Dynamics," *Econometrica*, Econometric Society, vol. 54(6), pages 1319-38, November 1986.

[41] Sherk, J. 2012. "Not Looking for Work: Why Labor Force Participation Has Fallen During the Recession." Backgrounder #2722, Heritage Foundation Center for Data Analysis.

[42] Shimer, R., "Why is the U.S. Unemployment Rate So Much Lower?" *NBER Macroeconomics Annual*, 13, pp. 11-61, 1998.

[43] Shimer, R., "The Impact of Young Workers on the Aggregate Labor Market," Quarterly Journal of Economics, 116, 969-1008, 2001.

[44] Shimer, R. "Reassessing the Ins and Outs of Unemployment," *Review of Economic Dynamics*, vol. 15(2), pages 127-148, April, 2012.

[45] Smith, C. "The impact of low-skilled immigration on the youth labor market". *Journal of Labor Economics*, 2012.

[46] Summers, L. "Why is the Unemployment Rate So Very High near Full Employment," Brookings Papers on Economic Activity, vol. 17(2), pages 339-396., 1986.

[47] Van Zandweghe, W. 2012. "Interpreting the Recent Decline in Labor Force Participation." Economic Review, Federal Reserve Bank of Kansas City, 5-34.